E

NOA MICAELA FIELDS

E

NIGHTBOAT BOOKS

NEW YORK

CONTENTS

HOMOPHONIC, TRANS LATER 1

E-1: ESTROGEN 3

ESTRADIOL (EXTRA DIAL) 5
ECHOLALIA 6
EMERGE 7
EXQUISITE CORPUS 8
EARS ARE AN EROGENOUS ZONE 9
ENDOCRINOLOGY 10
ESTROGEN 11
ECLIPSING BINARY 12
EULOGY FOR PAST SELVES 14

E-2: E~~A~~RASURE 15

ERRORS / EAR HARMONICS 17
ERR AND ECHO 18
EDGING 19
EAR-SPLITTING 20
ELLIPSES 22
DEAR E, RE: A— 23
EIDOLON 24
E FEELINGS 25
CATALYST, YOU 27
FIG. 8 28

E-3: ENTANGLEMENT 31

EQUALS DEATH 33
ENTROPY 34
ERUPT 35
ENOUGH! 36
EXODUS 37
ENJAMBMENT AS EMBODIMENT AS ESCAPE ART 38

E IS FOR EPIC 39
EPITHALAMIUM FOR U-HAUL LOVERS 40
EPIPHENOMENA 41
ENTANGLEMENT 42
EQUINOX 43

E-4: EXES 45

EVOCATION, EQUIVOCATION 47
EXES 48
EXCUSES 49
EROSION 50
EVERYTHING SAID AND DONE 51
ELEGY 52
EXIT MUSIC 53
ENDS 54

E-5: ECSTASY 55

E-6: ENDURANCE ART 65

ENDLESS 67
ENDURANCE ART 70
EVERY NIGHT 72
EVENTUALLY 73
ECHODISLOCATION 74

E-7: LOUISE 75

E DREAM 77
TELEPHONE 78
[ENABLE DREAM CAPTIONS] 80
LOUISE ZUKOFSKY LOST HER HEARING AID AT THE RAVE 81
EPILOGUE 84

NOTES: "A" INTO E 87

HOMOPHONIC, TRANS LATER

At the edge of hearing   *atmospheric strings*

Not a blank space   *Möbius strip*

Between sentences   *beginner's mindset*

My captionless life   *mea culpa*

What did I miss   *wander off-script*

Too embarrassed to ask   *dare embellishment*

Can you repeat that   *change of scenery*

Say again   *stray away*

I speculate spectrally   *isolated specks*

Consider possibilities   *conspiratorial syllables*

Ear transposes   *interrupting*

Jumbled syntax   *chamber music*

Risking wrong notes   *whistling one-way*

Periphery's poetry   *parallel play*

From other words   *form other worlds*

E-1: ESTROGEN

All night a hormone I pant

—Jos Charles

The poem is a hormone

—Lisa Robertson

IT WAS REALLY AN EXPERIMENT
IN POSING ALTERNATE WAYS
OF CONJUGATING MYSELF

—Juliana Huxtable

ESTRADIOL (EXTRA DIAL)

mishearing "A"-1 ["A / Round of fiddles playing Bach..."]

Arousal's unfaithful when played
back. I, uncanny daughter,
shapeshift buried libretto. Blasphemy!

Heads turn. Some can't bear
the diphthong overload,
clamorous decomposition.

My perverse meter of self
mutiny. I go on faggy
undefined dates and french

exit unless they enjamb
me in reverse pleasure.
A deeper connection.

So we're bookends.
Call me your trouble-
making twin, carrying

your music beyond recognition,
refrains substituted with detours,
surprise keychange leaps.

E decocts *A*'s tears.
Subtitles blink as I send
my counterfactual letters
to disco speech therapy.

When it's night I reconsider
what's cause and effect,
manuscript or girlhood?

I begin my reply with trills 〰
how art starts with haunting.

ECHOLALIA

mishearing "A"-19 ["An other / song—you / want another..."]

In other sounds
  E wants a mother
[unclear]   I hear

bad. Trachea,
  trace—translate
[hiss]   chase

meaning's
  severed half-
lives for cantos.

Mine pine
  after dorsal
fins. Drafts

drown in
  throat. I'm
pssst tense

subjunctive
  unfolding
spine, needling

form's tomb-
  narrow sonata.
Tingly

E taunts bow
  fingers dawn
lightly butchers

an author
  botches cadence
mutters in violet.

EMERGE

mishearing "A"-2 ["—Clear music—/ Not calling you names..."]

Cochlear mutation, contaminated art:
prophecy isn't meant to be stainless.
Unmuted *E* activates my spell
to catch the ghost of Louis Zukofsky.

A into E—there's risk
in surrogating *A*'s ballast, impaling with elisions.
Weight change, nausea, headaches, and/or mammary swelling...
I'm riding all the attractions today.

Odd revelations emerge when speech's choreography
defies the poet's intent. Through apocalypse
holed up, holding on, words climb out   [c l i m a x]

EXQUISITE CORPUS

mishearing "A"-8 ["Friends too tired to see differences, / This, Marx dissociated…"]

Frenzied, tongue-tied, dithering, this mouth-distorted sequel
prefers exquisite dissociation. Pivoting, E calls—
wants to mother. Bottomless the exploits
that created woman of man-
                                        y possibilities.

When dysphoria becomes faint memory
we will not disappear. Then we'll seesaw
from being a murmur to supernova.
Well, are you sure it's impossible
formally to think in goddess prose?
E's sublingual undertaking isn't obscene;
rewriting unburdens beauty.

It wasn't simple to part ways
with what I had internalized.
I suppressed my capaciousness.
Innocent mistake. Not to open honestly,
to smother what's original. As I practice
dematerializing, may dawn's light
spur me towards re-emergence.

And if it's true dissociation conceals prescient longing,
eventually I'll find my own way. Indiscrete
bodymind is capricious: a perfume, enigmatic
        prospect of seduction.

EARS ARE AN EROGENOUS ZONE

mishearing "A"-4 ["That our Psalms may reach but / One shadow of Your light..."]

Sedimented mirage body won't
shut off   up-late thoughts
dismay seeping   mind-altered   a weary mess

DANGER: groggy speech is promiscuous, promiscuous...

Tonight trans awaits your séance

Lust is restless and heightened
offering hounds feasts   I fear my heart
false starts
delayed love letters   off-hours temperance angel
reckless puberties of our desolation
split infinitive cartography
email the dead at dawn
autobiography can't avoid

**

Here she called for alien catachresis,
incongruous endorphins, empathogens:

Deafen us gods! Define us through the mystic
ouroboros   help us survive autotuned overtones
deus ex machinations
unreliably ourselves
demonstrative mouths ajar
rimming library

All I want is to mishear
your dead letters thrashing
shimmying sin til sunrise

When you come home shimmering
I'm quivering (giving in)

ENDOCRINOLOGY

mishearing "A"-13 ["Too heavy / for / my / breast pocket..."]

To hyphen form my breasts proceed

small tits as irises
I write, I revise

My thesis: A
vowel vibrates
off-course

by whole tones
now shuffling noticeably
who'll tell her

Doctor I prescribe
more iridescence

E's for misadventure
has moon in it
water too   wild

flowers cry hormones
when eyed by strangers

explain your spare parts

Part of me wonders
if this word
will let me in

subvert dealt name
I'll haunt someone else
consent to be ungovernable

ESTROGEN

mishearing "A"-12 ["The mind turns to the body..."]

That's my transgender body
inexperienced at noise
octaved isotopes all moshing

Deep dive
instar threshold
maxed out music

(E moves into short-circuitry)

Noa!
Shore's far?

Know what your body
can't do

Succumb to
waterbody canto

Orcas make rituals
of gestures
and disappear

ECLIPSING BINARY

mishearing "A"-12 ["MAN ⟶ EARTH ⟶ WORLDS"]

MOON ⟶ URGES ⟶ WORDS

Here we go
sapphic

|

speed-dialing
convulsions
overheard

|

alas crash
at last over
promising
headfirst
so long

What if
crush
ends with
withering

|

look out
amorous
thieves

|

replay
and replace

Redial
heed this
pursuit

|

breathe in
and begin
come clear

I AM NOT THE SAME
dear
you'll endure your eulogy

furthermore
if “his” story
  (heresy)
    ends here

caress her
  I carry on
becoming

1

binary

0 ____________

non-binary

V

B E

U R

S by narrating T

not by narrowing

` `

SELVES : theme
ASH : de/composition

EULOGY FOR PAST SELVES

mishearing "A"-12 ["Living, you love / So I love..."]

Laughing eulogy
so alive
wish threaded
innate through-
out untrue
further loving

——— *Telepathy*

Touch you ———

chimerical

After sainted boys fill

merry

new manuscripts he'll restart in the she

chart your sheets a palimpsest—my life

round

hollow dial tones out of synch, foreign

selves unite : free

go

Isomorphic tongue
made addressable by
undressing, blessing.

Art un
seeingly
hears us
at peace.

E-2: E~~A~~RASURE

My own body...
a determined echo   hammering away

—Chase Berggrun

no Book all stutters

—JJJJJerome Ellis

ERRORS / EAR HARMONICS

mishearing "A"-12 ["Blest / Infinite things / So many..."]

BLESS INFERNAL SYNTAX—
body piercings, sodomy, gender-switched
situationships, screwed up weekends...

To errors!
Ear harmonics, dial tones!

Unmatched romantic
starved by the pre-invented
        world, I amalgamate
                forms of various velocities,
                        madly modulating.

Whore death hears
all: stained pasts,
fractious words,
tongues opposed.

Wired clef, say what
now disasters
without strain.

Risk lessons:
will you understand
my all but fatal half
said "I love—"?

ERR AND ECHO

mishearing "A"-9 ["Its necessary nature, error ceases..."]

art follows ear and echo
—ERICA HUNT

Nascent erasures
ear cleaves
wrestling with nature.
Errors keep us

blurred *hush-BOOM*
deferred at will.
All enthralled by non sequiturs
entropy composes

inverting the leftover tune
cadenza silent, sis
abject conjoined titclaws
[*sic*] passing.

Syncopated future orchid
born through art
proprioceptive wounds
E ~~ffaced~~ book gone crying.

Indecipherable selves
swear by subtitles
thesaurus a la estradiol:
what a lustrous appellation.

EDGING

mishearing "A"-23 ["An album-leaf: on the Hill..."]

An abomination!
The holes gather
loose limbed dance
changes crisscross
across chasms   sing

Mishearings spring
vandalism vanishing a
long distance poem
forms different directions
  abrasive fresco

All the same—desire peels
 not forgotten, but forgiven

Parse these plosives
  bandaged hoarsely
pasting illegible notes
 sapphic overtones
ghost longing   fermata

Write in media res
overfamiliar gleaming
radiant monstrosities
lisp asking for trouble
   echodeviant art

Let unrest be atlas
practice killjoy fomentation
sobriquet interference
on fault lines still labile.
Implicated wrist, rewrite the rest

Reborn I'll glide :: unguarded angel
hide-and-seek pronunciation

Dear epidermis,
as Nomi grow

EAR-SPLITTING

mishearing "A"-23 ["An art of honor, laud..."]

On earth I must be LOUD
pleasuredome jaws cavernous incantatory sagas
fervently breaking escape velocity loquacious self-expansion.

O knock-off creators, no one forgives
  the pen's pantomime.
Why not be braless and lawless?

  you up? writing date?

I'm author now. Don't bother slipping on the horizon.
My noncompliant wordplay a switchy fantasy:
wounded animals wanting vice
                  versa wrong directions
named for ghosts we carry on lip-synching
seeking euphoria, untrained sensation.

Do re mi fashion respelled to justify
incipient selves far from earshot,
worried we'll miss the flight.
Incoming aberrations: verbatim or not,
  sing all detritus!

Until grammar embraces delirious
tonguelessness I'll risk entering
surrealism's dangerous cunnilingus.
Questing fingers rhyme pileup
gasps in no time.

Haven't you too whispered disclaimers
while lust-stricken? All I mean to say: stay
close / read between my lines.

When do I bare my trust, let you steer me?
Spillage madrigal implies I'm undaunted,
which (blushing) I'm only pretending.

Oopsy daisy you slurp my synonym
our covenant of whatever
you choose. Flip over—

if you want   sounds dreamy bb

Pillowtalk spills over
to exclamatory moaning.

Infinite Nomi: last seen
romancing infrasonic
where words backflip,
linger, fortune-tell.

E's song hollers back
devours A's reverie
nourishing faggotry.

ELLIPSES

mishearing "A"-7 ["Horses: who will do it? out of manes? Words..."]

Whores, let's bewilder our many verbs
willfully out of reach, I don't care. Most
days have no names, so we're argonauts. Blurred
adverbs frenzy together, muffing ghosts.
Forget haphazard, forget boyhood,
forget stubbled logic. Tribbing and I'm
homophonic, loudly TRANS UP TO NO GOOD!
Unreliable narrator I squirt an em
dash—compartmentalize while revisiting
cut ups. Fresh out of another relationship,
it's clear I'm not cut out for courtship.
You're cuuute though, no doubt we're corresponding.
I want to (do I?) pursue something new;
if I'm single too long I get stuck in a loop...

...honestly I'm pretty shifty. Won't belong
to anyone alone—I need my autonomy.
Come near but don't latch on too strong
or I'll be gone. Want to disappear with me
just for tonight, tie me up to the bedpost?
Leave me delirious, then let me loose my dear.
Let ellipses surround us like hopeful ghosts.
You know me, prone to mishear whatever I fear,
an enduring tentativeness that's hard to shake.
That's my queer orientation: words leaving wounds.
Tell me it's okay, how recklessly my heart aches
as I suffer for my art = life's expression.
No rehearsal, nor time for questions.
Can we change roles/letters/verbs, switch worlds?

DEAR E, RE: A—
mishearing "A"-22 ["Time vague gods intervals worlds..."]

> *A little softer, for what's been torn.*
> —Jada Renée Allen

Kindly disregard my internal whirlwind
neverlastingly stonewalled infinities
in the garden of wounds—erogenous
freefall with profuse apologies,
vacillating, reticence. Listen:
solitude's internal rhythms vary,
notwithstanding notebooks' narration
following memory's clouds, fishing
for all things approaching namelessness.

Diaries acknowledge terrifying passions,
making amends with thin noises [tender
to the touch, too emotional, inconsolable].
Won't you at least repair the page's lung,
this ingrown quicksand hungry for epiphany?
Lines for the end of time. A dangerous stanza
retaining some unfamiliar freedom.

I'm attached to fallible feelings, like how
the body streaks humiliation's excrement
in silence. No one will mistake desire
for a minor planet or prophet.

Only a forgotten vowel belies our elusiveness.

EIDOLON

mishearing "A"-13 ["You are not to throw out your music..."]

{ "Whose naughty art drowns out our music?"
seraphim whisper to one another }

Emasculated bosom of all breathing effervescences,
I trouble you for nothing but pray for a new skin [vibrational]
& undressing of intergenerational largo.
If I could segue, lapse, run-over...

Syntax the hormone
beak for misshapes   now the song's
disgraced out of tune   dirty talk
mystifying, wilting libido   asymptotic sissy
planting lewd hints to uncrossed dressers
offering myths, wanton apparitions
garbled toccata aftercare

>> SCINTILLATING CLOSE CAPTIONS AHEAD >>

I was so lost before E, self voyaged
away—illegible nomenclature
deferral grinding deviously allegro.

I sought to clarify what was obscure to me,
the words I disappeared inside of
at the gate of the mouth, irresolvably bodied.

I thank my mishearings, oracular guide.
How else could I recognize myself unseen?
Combinatorial conjectures full frontal.
If I had no mirror, a window: swung outward, so
I go.

E FEELINGS

mishearing "A"-5 ["A field behind brick wall, painted..."]

> *the **"e's"** turned slightly upwards—producing*
> *a feeling...that could only be felt with **"e's"***
> —KARI EDWARDS

A feeling beyond brick walls: painting
with mondegreen selves wiggling   r u b a t o

E feelings! E feelings! Mmm
ass against the art
dogged pursuit of the undefined
technicolor life outside
your laughable concepts of binaries.

A Family Scene

Assemble unfiltered fools
a rambunctious fiddle reunion

"—Why don't
I mark you?"

Candor:
do you think we are saying
anything new? our debris
propels in violent squawks
overshare reverb

Counter: barb chide forbid

[message unread]

No getting better I think
standstill | face to heart

Answer:
do you understand
daughter ambiguously defined
there's joy in change

Oh dear run off
with the poetry
my not so son
lick some sunlight

Fields
we're run-ons

CATALYST, YOU

mishearing "A"-17 ["Passer, deliciae meae puellae..."], a homophonic translation of Catullus 2

Pass ears delicately [my pulp hearing] :
spells of migraines, pleather, delayed migration...
Ok, I'll admit I dug through her secret diary
where she hummed to herself, figured narrow escapes,
suggestively reprinted the circumstances.
I wanted her stylish flair for drama. To come close.
Where's my dyke drama? Don't go running away!
I take care to itemize each depression chemically,
weed through stumped solicitations. Sorry.
Could my bottomless self risk your accidents,
bear ifs on late nights? Ready or not, here comes—

FIG. 8

I tried to mark the next shape of my body—
where it was going, if it would ever arrive
on the page, curl into another

name. Testing out a potential
respelling I practiced my new
would-be signature, cursive itineraries
accumulating in my

notebook. I spilled water so
the ink bled through, poetry
doodles and journal entries blurred.
I could see dissolving

traces of a book left behind
written by another self
I declined yet accepted as also partly
mine, crossed out or cramped
by annotations in my hand.

Here was my palimpsest—these
sedimented layers of sentimental
missives reminding me what I was

missing. Could I draw out
that unknowing I
felt? A draft

emerging on the page, a figure
eight, infinitely drifting from letter
to letter, outlining my course
through time or at least
my thinking and feeling
as pressed against the page,

enjambed. It was like how Renee Gladman
described drawing—what kept growing
as the hand moved, wanting some shape
"that looked like an *e* but was not an *e*
because of what the next shape was,"

the calamity of becoming
something else "un-alphabetic"
e losing its sense of

destination—and as I watch
Gladman's *e* changing
form, below the surface
e gradually rewires my body
and how I am feeling my way
out to meet the page.

E-3: ENTANGLEMENT

SO I CAN SLIP THROUGH THE TIGHTENING ENTANGLEMENTS

—Andrea Abi-Karam

to the many-handed hunger of transsexuality

—T Fleischmann

[   ] EQUALS DEATH

mishearing "A"-14 ["lower limit body / upper limit dance..."]
and "A"-12 ["I'll tell you. / About my poetics..."]

Hello, let me body
up here. Limbs dance
slower, plummet down.

Uppers lend speed,
lower inhibitions. SPEAK
UP! We're unamused.

Circlusion to alphabet the protest.

$$\int_{\textit{sick}}^{\textit{muzzle}}$$

What's integral?
Lower limit sick [silence]
Upper limit muzzle [mausoleum]

ENTROPY

mishearing "A"-10 ["Paris / Paris / Of your beautiful phrases..."]

Powerless parade
Pulse rising over brutal phrases
Residually haunted
Longing for tuning
Unfold divinations

Go ahead, poetess
Your work fuels derailed overtures
Notes for the protest
Incensed pronouns claws out

Cannot hear counterpoint
Cheated of a sense of momentum
Come over here, seer
Aporia offbeat brawling scoriaceous art
Outrun nomenclature's discolored parts
Insatiable freeform ghosts out of step

All people are POROUS
Make messes, refuse throats and thrones
Godmess with errors
Flat the sharps for a change
Chrysalis stereo

We're pariahs: replace the placards

ERUPT

mishearing "A"-8 ["Fresh as a daisy and as dirty..."]

Flesh acts I'm dizzy and I'm thirsting
for a faghagiography of ear
banditry. Opaque masochistic
tendencies out of place form
inverted expressive glossary.

Listen, what if—why not?—deependency
breaks capitalism's chords?

Sum of our stitched mouths compelled
to live with do-or-die prescience;
worked up, impatient with misspoken ridicule.

To what end will you personally proceed,
    or will you sign off on our forced deprivation?

Alternative: aleatoric message
for motion sick bottom feeders
morally impressionable; a spell-it-wrong
route to shepherd borderless bodies,
grasping verbs for unhoused questions
& adjectives for crepuscular
fight-or-flight states.

Here's where our struggles meet
            multitudinously, in
        transitive pillow talk.
So dream of desperados, glory
holes wherever we congregate.

                                    Erupt & drizzle
verdigris, too devastated to bloom
tuberose, masquerade wide awake.

All yesterdays loom on the edge of forgotten.

ENOUGH!
mishearing "A"-8 ["And this is repetition..."]

As for my reputation
drama queen incarnate
in any case unstable
our fallen angel stains
repaginating chapters ——— I bridge myself to Saint Anagram
(or was it Androgyne? Anyone?)
still I hope for your informed consent
to altar this shared dreambook of ours
endearing incunabulum

In any case I'm against rule following
don't own anything if you can avoid it
can't we already defund the prisons, pigs, and militia
these generous riots rephrase rage as wishes
what of yours is worth more than bearing
testimony to ongoing travesties?

EXODUS

mishearing "A"-12 ["This science of Mozart / Wreathing all instruments..."]

This silence admits the reach of our insulation.
Shaken out of tempo—tampering evident—
I'm enraged. Must speak what I'm not hearing.

Why does this seder feel impossible
          to pass over, if not now?

Miss on a meal enjoying freedom's song?
For what cost omit Israel's unceasing invasion?
Do we feast on complacent excuses
while complicit in denuding the Gaza strip?

"Anti-semitism," my brother called
our delaying of trains, hundreds in formation
against empire. Which left me
chanting NOT IN MY NAME.

So I'm the wicked child here
if I won't stop questioning
heartsore land fictions.
I'm averse to *dayenu*
when I've had enough.

How could I not resist
while across the table is hell,
terror, genocide? Forget never
again—we're parched eating tears
in order to observe Exodus.

ENJAMBMENT AS EMBODIMENT AS ESCAPE ART

mishearing "A"-6 ["And not performed till nine years later in Frankfort..."]

I'm not perforated tonight. Unrelated overheard
fragments my hearing aids pick up. And is my
protective hypervigilance audible
to others clocking our pharmaceutical
nerves, too sensitive for HRT?

    Beginner subtitles. Implausibly,
    categories degrade- - -
    now please understand
    the truth's unenviable.

Hell's re-elected and making a cacophony
(as if he ever left us). Hey
confidant, do you have time
to drop by? I'm tearing up too much.

How should I hurl
self's newest design? Blackout forgive her

I won't forget what you said:

            Can't desire
            for the future
            be trans? Veer
            to prophecy?

    And even if

                penis comma

Weather this murkiness
make art that escapes.

E IS FOR EPIC

Everywhere We Look, There We Are
—Cameron Awkward-Rich

Licentious initiation: hands of a sutured sister's future lover guide me into the musty backroom of the gay library. This is romantic friendship: always just two degrees of separation in the T4T daisy chain. I'm looking for queercore punk zines. Pull out a box of zines by Fertile La Toyah, better known as Vaginal Davis, the terrorist drag name she gave herself in homage to Angela Davis. Here is *shrimp*, her one-off foot fetish zine from the 90s. Turned-on turning through pages. Caption: "LOOK AT THE CUTE PROTESTOR."

Vaginal Davis was still living in LA in the nineties when I grew up there but we wouldn't be in the same room until decades later in Chicago. I was in the audience at her artist talk with my roommate who knew her from Berlin, affectionately enough to pick up nickname: "the dainty satanist." Not that these biographical facts matter really but proximity is the archive's wet dream, cumstains on the page a palimpsest of touch, prior touching, a private connection to the past hooking the present and future to a slanted lineage. Now get thee to a xerox machine, copy some pages. "E IS FOR EPIC!"

(An epic poem for our epicene epoch? Not to equate my E and hers but maybe we're talking about the same thing, at any given time we might be on estrogen or ecstasy or both, twin blue pills under the tongue and the Blue Mondays after. A library of tears, dysphoria dissolving lifetimes away via misbegotten rites of passage. Meanwhile we write and rewrite passages of cruising shadows, a different story every night.)

Right after this I have a date at Nobody's Darling who indulges my overeager play-by-play over drinks then confesses that they are in the process of ritually excommunicating the letter E from their life following a recent divorce, because their ex-wife's name starts with an E. I offer to take E off their hands. So we take off to their place, swap vowels for the night.

EPITHALAMIUM FOR U-HAUL LOVERS

mishearing "A"-2 ["Half-human, half-equestrian, clatter of waves..."]

As you move-in androgynously, closet-swap,
fabulate secret love blessings, if you
never oppose desire's bracing threshold,
tilt towards one another's moonmoons,
your laughter will stay warm, open
love within love → full-grown.

As some philosopher advised,
let everyday life become a work of art
—in bed. If there's no one way
we're supposed to live our days,
go mosey in the flowers, trade
smoky alley kisses, leap after life.
Rearrange furniture promiscuously
in pursuit of delight,
then break in the space
at a daring pace, settle into
a new center of gravity,
be muses to each other.

It is not obscene
to crush at high speed, go on
a first date lasting forever, never leave...
unstoppable T4T love.

EPIPHENOMENA

mishearing "A"-3 ["At eventide, cool hour..."]

We're dyeing our clothes eerie black
mirroring the full moon's splotches
frisky post-hallucinatory
roommate ritual offering
belletrists apostrophizing
our many-named cats

                                        Overlap
witchily for instance just past
midnight we're both at Midway
back from separate trips
on delayed rescheduled flights
by happenstance share a ride
home how'd we manage that
our lucid luck   I say auspicious

Trust what's close aligned
parallel homophone windfall rhapsody
synchronized hysterics :: ghost orgy

Co-write a journal to practice
durational collaboration
almost incestuous punctuation
make of me a hyphen mark
living side by side

ENTANGLEMENT

mishearing "A"-15 ["He could not think another..."]

We cook up schemes, co-conspire
in anticipation of symbiosis. Laughing,
enamored with another world
we instantiate when we're together;
but we misstate our revolution's stakes
if we omit our encompassing
community. An incomplete gesture
I suppose, maintenance art to care
despite antagonism's demagogy.

Mutual muse terrorism: simply put,
hyphenation demands we synch up
collectively, an army of fools
co-parenting haphazard realities
without precedent, with only pervasive
goodwill and curiosity. So we befriend
our neighbors who've seen more
than we could ever understand
before we crashed in. Ask
more from each other. As much
as we can, insist on resistance's
imperative and let it steadily alter us,
permeate our relationship discussions
and other mundane rituals, compel us
to act and to gather with urgency,
prescience, and courage of mind.

Here's to our entanglement, my dear—
with each other and the rest of the earth,
abundance in our maximalist home   the Pervert Kitchen.

EQUINOX

misbearing "A"-15 ["No lady Rich is very poor..."]

Melodies, wishes, there we go—
seasons we're always morphing,
sweeping through the major arcana,
weathering earth-broken hearts,
high-maintenance placements.

Our apartment's right this way—
outliers enthroned
at the threshold of rumor.
Weirdo interdependence;
unkempt lepidoptera live here.

Fusion of pansy siblings
who flaunt the will to lip sync,
our Wellbutrin recital instigated
by the obscene boyfriend parade,
neuroses ("new roses?") on the loose.

I'm overly forgiving by default.
Like knocked-over coffee.
"All's ephemeral."
"Dogma of friendly death."
"Sounds pheromonal."

Notoriously we're hyperbolic
in the naughty clairvoyant loading zone.
Words crossdress trashily,
thrown together in ad hoc collective,
our prefigurative drafting.

I dog-eared the page asking,
Have you assembled y/our anatomy yet?
And yes, we are otherwordly.

E-4: EXES

An Army of Ex-Lovers Cannot Fail
—Lesbian Herstory Archive

and for the lovers who found a mirrored heart
they just remind me I'm without you
—FKA twigs

EVOCATION, EQUIVOCATION

mishearing "A"-22 ["now summer happy new year..."]

Nuisance in our half-finished ear:
so many tongues of yours
sewn of paper
lick mourning stains.

Bisexual music downpour
drag of saying too much
for thought to reach by feel.

What troubles all lovers
is needing to trans
late to relate much less elate—
collisions inevitably erupt.

Important to remember:
a lover's bed's not empty
watch for ghosts who interrupt.

Boys in motion love to
dilute promises   lend
a sense of collusion
to all antonyms.

Fouls inscribed in tears
begging for idolatry foreplay;
we'll forgive them all later.

EXES

Tone(-deaf) row mishearing "A"-20 ["Ecce puer / for a dancer..."]

Echo poor
Sporadic answers
Paraphrase Noa Fields
Palinode whenever
Spillover poet pronoun improvisation
Vagabond shapeshifter
Cruising ampersands for sex
Troublemaking double entendres
Oblivious to suggestion
Paradox selves third wheel
Trespass consonants vicariously
Subtext carelessly

Third Street palms swaying
A coast view   exes pool
Vexing Thanksgiving ends in group sex
Somehow a ménage à trois I double back
Act out the subjunctive's unintended sapphics
Subtitles for repressed distant memories
Threesome forms uneasy chorus
Peripheral metamour conjunction
Perpendicular   simple geometry
Forms dangling

Vague crush harbinger
Vibes politely pursued posthaste
"We" disproportionately accommodating
Full of dissonance
Cross-wired chemistry
Threatens lovers' tremolo
Emotional hard-on
Sub seeking puncture
Parenthetical next to you
Compromising positions
Tremulously held onto

EXCUSES

mishearing "A"-5 ["'You write a strange speech.' 'This.' / One song / Of many voices..."]

"You alright?"   Estranged, speechless.
                              Once done, unmentioned.

Voyage these wounds my love.
Weep, pang—call declined.
        Barbed dedication
    undermined a life with you.

I say words have needs
        warring in them, fault junctures.
                (New Year's, thin ice, the rattling fight
                with the freight of our trouble)

Perplexed clauses
cheaters choose through tears:
"I blew someone in the steam room."
On our date night?
Can't sleep, guard's up.
Night of exposure, exhausted
détente come-hither
—and love? Blew me over and over.

EROSION

mishearing "A"-9 ["An impulse to action sings of a semblance..."]

Impulsive you'd act
on assonance often
belatedly befuddle

vows. But the moment I call you
his—I'm left inconsolable.

Would it do me good to keep
disemvoweling, I ask you
hardly near sure
what I'm losing once more.

So there was the sting
of what words couldn't say,
like how unlikely love
was when we met. I meant,

my ~~he~~art remainders our exchanges.
But how do I hold onto your voltage?

Volta: we flee (*write* it!)
the people who made us.

EVERYTHING SAID AND DONE

mishearing "A"-6 ["Because I believe I can do more good that way…"]

Speed dial. Belly laugh. I can't
dump your ghost. I hate you.

Thanks anyway.

Index cards in hand I scribble
all our pasts and futures. Cross out.

Now it's almost all indecipherable.

Not present. Abusing generosity.
Standoffish. Straying. Irreproachable.
Wounded booty calls. Inevitably.

Call your sobering up a process,
not sheepish appeasement.

Eventually strong. No more calls, reaching out.
I will throw away everything we wrote out.

ELEGY

mishearing "A"-11 ["River that must turn full after I stop dying..."]

Written: that I must thorn, fall apart...
I'll stop trying to string songs
outracing grief all night. My love
for self-destruction: a fortnight of sob
stories. Thrown away keepsakes and my senses
dismiss the foregoing frayed pieces.

Human onwards, darling.
Who's lossless? Show me a wish unimpaired.
Taped-together wings, sorry state of affairs.
Glaze your teardrops, each one's nurturing
lived-in fables to urge on unstapled hearts.
Go on, maze these wefts of feelings.
Art needs hurdles, reversals. Strap in
angel. By chance hear singing
when the dial tone rings—there's fingers
(hold) pressing me along.

EXIT MUSIC

mishearing "A"-8 ["And out of respect for what he said about Bach..."]

Out of self-respect, forget about getting him back.
I need to move on >> search inward.
Rewind << study love's mistakes
and when you pine, think through
the consequences, before—

hey just reaching out

First the flirting
unpurposeful play
repressed desires resurface
somehow sucked in.

How'd we get here?
Joined by a pulse
for madder music
replaying disaster
oh there we go again
in spite of alternatives
internalizing Da Capo
succumb to forsworn pair.

Two nightly confounded
swallow better intentions
not to sleep together.
But by daylight we will
admit this is good
bye (I mean it).

ENDS

mishearing "A"-24 ["And it is possible in imagination..."]

VIOLIN I — Ends, if impossible, unimaginable
VIOLIN II — I can't trust "there there" mimetic hit-and-run mouth
VIOLA — (Poet finds she doubts words; hysterical negations
CELLO — History: *E* is a storage unit of mine blast off infinity clauses

Too divorced speed of all-grown-up illuminations
I'd rather detune a fiddle
form sidereal time) in a writhing tempo
not to fall through time (somatic wishes)

The lessons begin emotions off-shore
less lust let roses, glitches
admissions of the hidden mind butt in
confused if we're on the same page I fly back for the weekend

Ideas, migraines mistakes, more mistakes
"A" rings rings rings to a close
I did not want to break up
Together: noise

E-5: ECSTASY

ecstatic craft of the living body
—Duriel E. Harris

ecstasy is queerness's way
—José Esteban Muñoz

Wildness found her   (she never had to look far)
looking so comma spliced tonight
pain's elective, pen's elastic
stumbling around the warehouse
rave staring down paradise

And she splinters at will
animal   milestone   gyrating
    between men sweating
 max-embodied syntax
bellowing astonished

    NO ONE'LL BELIEVE I FEEL THIS

                Weekend soulmates,
                let's go and escape

Whimsical tunnel visions
dilated pupils tune in
she stays out all night
set for the ride

As ecstasy defenestrates her
moves her up a pitch
she lets loose a moan

                                        aaaaaaaaaahhhhhhh

Journey laced with heresies
sprawled over the beats
I too was bursting
                    inertia demon

Deluge swept up in debasement
    wade the flesh dance
halting pickup lines misunderstood
ghost sweat in darkrooms
                    naughty excess

Ecstasy till sunrise, c'mon—
melt into the unrestrained dancefloor
reverb frenzy needing to stray further
then who shows up but *that* ex

Devil's wish to block out desire
grapple with the undefined
but since hurt lacquers foolish vices
desire lunges for putrefaction

Enema stylus   nightlife [write the rites]
Bottoms dread diminuendo
                                        Uh!

Single let loose, edging, brimming—
            obscene unearthing

    sub breaks a sweat   threesomes
                                      cum forth

Key: depart assdeep homage pagination
in case of coven emergency phallo-sonic rumination
I don't want to be present when night purges her song

Here tell of self-medication
adderallshroomsempathogensweed

Once longed for
ampersand leakage
now indecent art
"arse poetica"   (harvest us)

Naaaasty Nomi
enunciate queerly

E's a crowdpleaser
the motive goes

||: d i e s i s :||

(atonal sister)

distraught liebestraum leaves me
rapt -
ur a round

decenter me

Anxiously seen
through the doors descending
clockable viscera

As for those who're into mistake rituals
or swear by cyclical excess
wounds wildplay sleepless
mouth your hands' secrets selfsame form

Descry [unnamed]
now morphing *K anybody?*

Striptease roman a clef
see through yours

Indeterminate my fallowing
I saga nowhere

If I'm inside a washroom
        it's awash with noise
etymologically who am I?

Get out of here
blinking I em dash

Then I'm a self-abandoned
meteorite (which you told me
are really lovelorn)

                Yet I danced, stayed

                        Sorry for your baggage

Tender a new with
-drawn me weathering off hours

                                        Were you fought after

            Meet me halfway since
            fortune told italicized crying

                                                Hey man, don't cry

I dance, séance
a chimera now

We're wishing nowadays
o peace as I safely go

                    You seem as if already dead

How many times was I
bestiary?

Overheard: *pansy, suck my dick*
then *boy or girl?* hysteria

Vicarious chorus of obscenities
which my (dis)appearance brought on

my self   aberrant
scanning   broken stanzas
disturbance   bruised

Hear lies yours truly
knocked out
dying myths
cemented rumors

In other words:
we will not matter

Flood hindsight   music
arousal's feral swaying
weather a fist
asymptote she flees hands foreign tonight
E screams   smudge overfeelings
naughty gender fiction appeals
fetal grunt
asked eons before
mutant loving no place
not trying and loving no face

Now calling to pester pent-up fears
perhaps she'll choose fangs to dismember
terror deterrent tactic
trickster agitprop

Moan wet regret
soaked in orphaned orifices
insoluble ditto marks
besides herself in spite

A final wish:
re-release our ends, severed by love

Aching in books
Cunt pulsating
Grave golden shower
To mourn or to moan
Wanting to be well again

Still waking, sleep-bothered
Wet glottis, tits itch
You ask yourself why
Fear owns your body

What you're wanting at all hours:
Grow up → survive

Write: *Wildness found her...*

E-6: ENDURANCE ART

But all must be endured, since . . .
—Sappho, tr. Diane Rayor

I KEPT MYSELF ALIVE
—Tehching Hsieh

ENDLESS

mishearing "A"-14 ["beginning An..."]

beginning end

b*end*
unhinged I
assume form
pulpy
wet
cursive
dithering
perforated
feral
overt
inconstant
wilting
foreplay
hocket
titrate
pleasure
moan low
blast late
he
pleased
pees
bosom
simpers
thirst for ill-
loved poems

begging end
unsayable
come misprint
smelling vulgar
paddle sex
to light
like some
body else's
uncovered
tonight

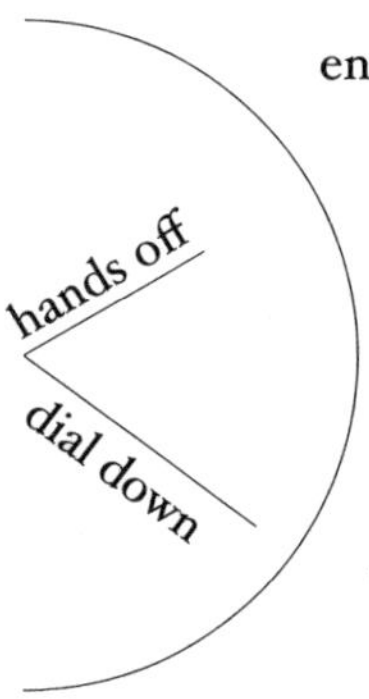

enough

the hours

plenty

for all

the ditto

wound
up you
couldn't wait
would you
breathe out
doubt called
ghost backwards

undo
mouth how
steep is trust
cleaved howl
distant somewhere
hurt invaginated
when dissociating
went where
hell asked
for increased vigil
ance\stress syllables
furtively in grave
a maze
erased
am I
gone anywhere?
will I
half-begun
end?

ENDURANCE ART

mishearing "A"-23 ["An unforeseen delight a round..."]

When after she desired a sound
begging inarticulate to emptied
prescient letters moshing hives
a wound worn inwards
happenstance prompted histrionics,

after she curled warbling
rock-bottom cantos overworked
low skies wolfish possessive
composite creature/creator tottered
between languages shedding,

after its anguished concerto
flared up hearing calamity
midwest bruises interminable
she wanted no more successive
mirror scars went on sertraline,

when hurting while hurtling
with barebacked forgetfulness
syntax moving licentiously
ignore destiny confide fallback
kleptomaniac disorientation,

toward perpetual outburst
stoned out of focus
delirium loves less treble
foreground chirographic
choreography of escapism,

asterisks she survives all-
iterates dodging turnstiles
several nightlives later
ovulation envy
cathects to lacerating liaisons,

subwoofer laughter as likely
as designer name dropping
when end rhyme's overpriced
each call back sisyphean
width lengthening what's never complete,

progesterone holy dalliance:
feel hormones reach her (weren't we
already unconsciously audible?)
trust in adjacency, sisterhood
cheers to alibis some gratified

entering haphazard next moves
to suspend reality expand worlds
we're ethereal write that down
sporadic throughlines
ruminate promise more.

EVERY NIGHT

mishearing "A"-21 ["Free. I am fain Fane / old word pun..."]

3am: pain's pane
holds worse punishment
frenzied operatic night-yearning
shakes door frame
plots undiplomatic schemes
suggests atemporal kinks
dalliances poor us
we *had* it all
drywall gamblers
risk-averse prophecy
not tonight I might someday
not tonight I might climb
into the nearest heart
                                        awake

EVENTUALLY

mishearing "A"-2 ["I walked on Easter Sunday..."]

I'll wake up easier someday
kissing a face
facing kismet

Paraphrase: I'll wait out predawn
for analogue lovers
if only a tryst could comfort
assure meaning in a striptease treatise...

Write after
buoyant girl cruising abstract
forms not yet known gay-imbued horizon
feels vast potential in breast to love
flying close ∞

Could that be my gossipy future?

—but troubadours assign at berth
trials to mock our weaknesses
for the fun of it (UNFORTUNATE)

Oh go save yourself, bless us out of this vocabulary.

ECHODISLOCATION

mishearing "A"-16 ["An / inequality..."]
and "A"-17 ["Anemones / 'But we ran ahead of it all..."']

I'm
irresolvably

in flux

*

Animals at best
we've run holoalphabetic
A-Z eventually language
irrepressibly intricate syntax
an unpronounceable crescendo

Needs buried improperly
perplexed fuming too remorseful
misheard his agenda
as if inside out

E-7: LOUISE

Death, yet my woman's mind
trembles thru me,
("*A*"-21)

Louise
Set in the glacier
("*A*"-13)

E DREAM

Heretic, according to hearsay
I was raving by your graveside
illuminated by an elusive blue moon
when you arrived kicking up dust,
my exquisite corpse correspondent
live in the flesh with a confession:
you're on estrogen in the afterlife,
which by the way is bursting
with lesbian bars you like to frequent
where you scribble poems on napkins
you'll read to anyone who'll listen. I ask
if you chose another name in the end,
you tell me you've picked up an *e*—
"Call me Louise."

TELEPHONE

Louise writes homo
phonic poems re
mixing Catullus
with her wife
Celia “mea lesbia”
dyke soundalikes
tongue slipping south
from sound as found
to something fecund.
Tumbling out of the same
mouth shapes as if
his mouth were hers—
easy to confuse
wanting someone
with wanting to be
someone so much
so desire distorts
sense and the senses
blur. Language
fails to report
how it feels to bend
the self to another
possibility so near.
Something about
these poets’ poly
glottal drag
calling back
to my mind
playing telephone
as a child. Whispers
passed around a
circle a secret
message kept
shifting in between
mouth and ear.

When it came to me
I felt the heat
in my ear
a rush of air
too soft too hard
to understand.
The shapes forming
in my mouth
didn't make sense
so I phoned it in.
I didn't mind
cutting out
if language could
be my own
private I don't know.

{ENABLE DREAM CAPTIONS}

> In need of captioning and tired of waiting for access I take matters into my own hands and transcribe.

> Who better to caption than the hard of hearing? Call me amanuensis to the vibrating whorl of our hypervivid present, sight reading the half-lives of objectivist archives for futureform.

> Behold: I am the autonomous captioning service top mouth of disappointment which is freedom of movement which is the wish fulfillment fantasy of cruel optimism.

> What if our ears met each other like mouths opening for a kiss? Let's pitch shift the dream ritual, scissor the vowels.

> From the jump my captions are fallible. The better to fall fast and hard for. Watch me flirt with the dictionary. We're both shape shifting in real time and we improvise towards transposed mutual misunderstanding.

> So what if my version is not an annotation? It's a callback to what was already between the sheets, I mean the lines.

> Louise Zukofsky was a technobottom. I saw her at the rave last weekend right up front by the dj, rubbing against the subwoofer. Boom boom! She leaned in to say something, I couldn't catch the words but I followed the lip action, entranced.

LOUISE ZUKOFSKY LOST HER HEARING AID AT THE RAVE

mishearing "A"-22 ["AN ERA / ANY TIME / OF YEAR..."]

Unhear me out errant lovers!
I'll share my summer languish,
an account of undiscerning ears. A
night out with friends at a party,
oblivion on the dance floor,
shadows on the wall commingling.
Trans math of self-pitying neurons
til rooftop weed rewires—great,
I'm open to opening up.

Association creates worlds. Nightlife
unfastens solitudes: dare, reach, turn.
Leads me on, limbs heretic.
Sleepless night owls endure
nonstop to forget whatever
else is shared between friends
wide-eyed, washed out.

Deep in how we're dizzy
beneath our participatory glamor
when we ampersand, dance.
For me it's about trust. Spinning
with my noisy muses I conduct
myself good-naturedly, spiritedly
breaking in the weekend when
beep beep beep my battery's dead
so I stash my hearing aids
in my purse, safe and sound
while I dance the night away.

An error, if ever there was one,
my delinquent bacchanal, forgetful
of intent's loose initiative.
Sure enough, when I break
for air, drained, I notice
one ear's gone missing.
Where on earth could it be?

Stumped I retrace my hours,
aware how unlikely it is
to reappear. I edge shadows
zigzagging with the flashlight
on my phone. One raver wonders
what I'm looking for,
leading to a flurried but fruitless
search party. Call it a night?
"I work here," he tells me.
"What's your number? If
we find it, we'll call you."
Now I forfeit my case,
rack my brain pacing home
sweating the cost of a replacement.

Belief only ever lets you down.
Sure, miracles occasionally find
someone deserving of a makeover;
but is this assistance from above,
or instances in a vacuum,
recorded for posterity's dubious heirs
to assuage aching hearts?
Please! I'd rather find another
fallback before spiraling down
that path, buoyed by impractical
allegory. Who can afford that?

Look: the moon's up, looking
up somewhere above earth
even as we're sinking. I'm comforted
in the morning by a wake-up text:
turns out daylight had unearthed
what I figured hopelessly lost
when the party was done
and the organizers cleaned up!
I withdraw my disbelief,
my stray hearing aid found
grazing the loveseat (third floor)

and returned to me, wayward
instrument outlasting expectation,
apparently awaiting our reunion.

Here ends, irrefutably, my scrapped
soapbox sob story. It seems
we've conjured a miracle—I'm swayed,
repainted sane, if startled
by wish-fulfillment in writing.
We are caught in our unknowing;
bewildered, take heart in our hurtling art.

EPILOGUE

mishearing "A"-10 ["The snake / Rings communications…"]

With a guitar and an E string that sticks to itself.
—TC Tolbert

Troublemakers, can we agree mistakes are sacred
wings?

Some say words are such local menaces
however entirely rewritten
adolescents remain careenagers.

Sister scribes I tell you:
if we're intersecting
it's time to loop
the tale and glue it back on,
an endless round playing.

Dare overwrite, about-face.
Forget hymn and teleport
to the legato——
trans accomplishment.

NOTES: *"A"* INTO *E*

I picked up a battered copy of Louis Zukofsky's doorstopper *"A"* from the dollar bin at my neighborhood bookstore-cum-apothecary, Space Oddities (RIP). Over five decades, Zukofsky poured music, family drama, Marxist politics, and autobiography into his "poem of a life." When I saw that the cover page was all but torn off, I knew that I would put it to use as an "alterbook" (change is sacred). My roommate and I were always looking for material to alter, collage, and reimagine. I drew a big anarchist "A" over the title page and recorded my erasures and mishearings in the margins.

What I call "mishearings" are inspired by homophonic translation, a form which latches onto the sounds but not the meaning of a mother text, like a game of telephone gone haywire. (Many thanks to my teacher Mónica de la Torre, who introduced me to the form.) Zukofsky practiced homophonic translation within *"A,"* as well as in other projects with his wife Celia, mimicking the sounds of passages from Catallus's poems in Latin. But my own interest in homophony, as a hard-of-hearing poet, is as a subversive tool to experiment with mishearing's expansiveness. I sought to recuperate hearing loss as a site of generative crip and trans imaginings. My associative meanderings, made with the glitchy companionship of my hearing aids, felt like a process of divination.

Transposed up a fifth, *E* sings *"A"* in a new key altogether—estrogen, that powerful feminine life-force. In echo, *E* revealed itself as a portal for transformation, a space to inscribe and archive the process of my transition. Like my body on the hormones I was beginning to take as I wrote this book, the poems drifted towards themselves. In the name of metamorphosis, liberation, and unruliness, I stopped looking back at the source text and took liberties in shifting lineation or further mishearing my own mishearings. The sum of these drafts document a corporeal process of drift and growth across five years of writing and revising.

During this time I kept finding *e*'s everywhere, as if haunted by the vowel. At the Gerber/Hart Library and Archive, I found a Vaginal Davis zine crowing "E is for epic!" That same night I went on a first date with a recent divorcee who was trying to expel the letter *e* from their life, the first letter of their ex-wife's name. But later an even more surprising *e* jumped out at me within the covers of *"A"*: "The tourist emerald of Lake Louise, / Set in the glacier."

When I saw "Louise," my imagination ran with her as a feminized renaming of my predecessor. Suddenly I pictured an afterlife of Louis Zukofsky on E, becoming a trans woman. My sissification of an author I love, however irreverent it may come across, is intended as homage. In the slippery tradition of New Narrative, I made Louise into a time-warped alter ego, placing her in scenes from my own life, like the time I lost a hearing aid at a rave. Not only do the sounds of our poems phase in and out of each other, but our lives criss-cross on the page as mischief-making twins.

Beyond the book you hold in your hands, *E* has taken on additional lives through multimedia collaborations, including videos, sound pieces, and performance rituals. I see this (ongoing) profusion of *e*'s as a palimpsest—timestamps of a body of work in the works, always becoming. *E* is not fixed, and so comes with an invitation: while I have my own attachments to the language in this book, I welcome (caring and deliberate) misreading or mishearing, especially by other trans, queer, and disabled kin. If that is you, please feel free to remix the text in this book as a departure point for your own exploration and self-narration, or even collaboration.

*

In "Errors" the phrase "the pre-invented world" comes from *Close to the Knives: A Memoir of Disintegration* by David Wojnarowicz..

The title of the poem "Dear E—Re: A" is from a letter Louis Zukofsky wrote to Ezra Pound in 1930, which proceeds: "How shall I begin? You see-saw my heart ups and downs."

In "Fig. 8" the phrase "that looked like an *e* but was not an *e* because of what the next shape was" comes from Renee Gladman's *Calamities*.

"E is for EPIC": I accessed Vaginal Davis's zine *shrimp* at the Gerber/Hart LGBT Library and Archives in Chicago. A PDF scan can be found online on the Digital Transgender Archive.

The line "Let everyday life become a work of art" in "Epithalamium for U-Haul Lovers" comes from *Everyday Life in the Modern World* by Henri Lefebvre, translated by Sacha Rabinovitch.

In "Erosion" the parenthetical injunctive "(*write* it)" samples Elizabeth Bishop's poem "One Art."

"Ends" uses musical staff notation, inspired by Celia Zukofsky's innovative setting of her husband's words to Handel's chorale score in *"A"*-24, a gift for his 64th birthday. She quotes from his poetry, fiction, drama, and essays on different voice lines. In my version, I rearranged the misheard lines as a string quartet with stanzas which can be read as four concurrent voices reading. My brothers, mom, and I make up a full quartet, and we grew up playing chamber music together.

E-5: Ecstasy composites mishearings of the following fragments from "*A*": ["white flower she / so long as sleep...] ("A"-12); ["A German lady there said..."] ("A-1); ["An animate still-life —night..."] ("A"-5); ["Natura Naturata—/ Nature as created..."] ("A"-6); ["Go, / Beg His Corpse..."] ("A"-3); ["The blood's tide like the music..."] ("A:-1); and ["a queen in Bucks County..."] ("A"-12). The line "NO ONE'LL BELIEVE I FEEL THIS" is lifted directly from "A"-12 (all-caps mine).

Telephone: "mea lesbia" quotes Catullus 5, a lover's ode.

In "Epilogue," I borrow the neologism "careenagers" from Louis Zukofsky's novel *Little (for careenagers)*— dedicated to his violin prodigy son, Paul Zukofsky.

"[Enable Dream Captions]" references "cruel optimism," the late queer theorist Lauren Berlant's description of desire's punishing self-relation.

ACKNOWLEDGMENTS

With gratitude to the publications who housed earlier versions of these poems, including:

Action, Spectacle: "Err and Echo," "Endless," and "Evocation, Equivocation"

Anomaly: "Ellipses" and "Ear Splitting"

Antiphony: "Exquisite Corpus"

Oxford University Press: my article "Dropping E at the Death Club" co-authored with Marke Bieschke included "Ecstasy" and "Louise Zukofsky Lost her Hearing Aid at the Rave"

Tripwire: "Estrogen," "Errors/Ear Harmonics," "Err and Echo" (previously titled "Earasures"), "Emerge" (previously titled "Evolution"), and two fragments "Ecstasy" and "Expletive" from what would become E-5: ECSTASY

Tyger Quarterly: "Early Exit" (another fragment from E-5) and "Ends" (previously titled "The Effraction of Alterity")

Zoeglossia: "Echolalia," which was later reprinted in Poetry Foundation's Poem of the Day

Thanks to my godsend editor Gia Gonzales, who always knew just what was needed to fix the book, and the entire Nightboat team: Emily Bark Brown, Stephen Motika, Lindsey Boldt, Kit Schluter, Lina Bergamini, Dante Silva, and Morgan Levine, who were a dream to work with on my first book. Thank you Sofia Moreno for your beautiful art gracing my book cover.

Endless thanks to the writers, mentors, teachers, friends, lovers, exes, sisters, collaborators, and other family chosen and blood, who shared space in writing groups and classrooms, in DIY spaces, at protests and on dance floors, who made this book possible and even more, enabled my writing selves throughout my evolutions, including (but not limited to—oh forgive my omissions, give my love to anybody): TC Tolbert, Ryan Greene, Stefania Gomez, Rosemary Spring Wexler, Riley Yaxley, Stevie Cisneros Hanley,

MMM, Mahnu, Maya Nguyen, Mariposa Divina, Madeleine LeCesne, Jared Brown, Chrysanthemum Tran, Aza Greenlee, AJ McClenon, Ruby Que, Erika Ordos, Armando Lozano, Ulrich Baer, S. Yarberry, Odette Stout, Eva Geczy, Warren Walters, Emily Mar Garcia, Alexx Novy, Adam Sackman, Andrea Abi-Karam, Roque Salas Rivera, Ari Banias, Joss Barton, Ava Mirage, Syd Staiti, Violet Spurlock, Jamie Townsend, Travis Alabanza, Samuel Ace, Vaginal Davis, Ed Roberson, Julian Talamantez Brolaski, Mónica de la Torre, E. Rowan Mena, JJJJJerome Ellis, danilo machado, Carole McCurdy, DFBRL8R Gallery, Disability Lead, Guild Literary Complex, No Nation Tangential Unspace Lab, PO Box Collective, Poetry Foundation, Trans/Space is Expanding, Trans Vengeance, and Zoeglossia. And finally: special thanks to the E that bore me, my mother, Elizabeth Fields.

Noa Micaela Fields is a trans poet with hearing aids. She lives in Chicago. www.noamicaelafields.com

ISBN: 978-1-64362-293-4

Cover art: "Demonio blanco como cautivo haciéndose pasar por una mujer"
by Sofia Moreno (mixed media, 9cm x 28cm, 2023)

Design and composition by Kit Schluter
Typeset in Hoefler Text

Cataloging-in-publication data is available
from the Library of Congress

Nightboat Books
New York
www.nightboat.org

NIGHTBOAT BOOKS

Nightboat Books, a nonprofit organization, seeks to develop audiences for writers whose work resists convention and transcends boundaries. We publish books rich with poignancy, intelligence, and risk. Please visit nightboat.org to learn about our titles and how you can support our future publications.

The following individuals have supported the publication of this book. We thank them for their generosity and commitment to the mission of Nightboat Books:

Kazim Ali • Anonymous (4) • Ava Aviva Avnisan • Jean C. Ballantyne • Will Blythe • Rob Byrnes • V. Shannon Clyne • Theodore Cornwell • Gisela Gamper • Photios Giovanis • Amanda Greenberger • David Groff • Daniel Handler • Sarah Heller • Karen Holtzman • Parag Rajendra Khandhar • Katy Lederer • Shari Leinwand • Daniel Levine • Elizabeth Madans • Ricardo Maldonado • Pooja Mehta • Ethan Mitchell • Claudia Morgan • Caren Motika • Elizabeth Motika • Asker Saeed • The Leslie Scalapino - O Books Fund • Amy Scholder • Thomas Shardlow • Eric Suchyta • Benjamin Taylor • Mohan Trivedi • Jerrie Whitfield & Richard Motika • Clay Williams

This book is made possible, in part, by grants from the New York City Department of Cultural Affairs in partnership with the City Council and the New York State Council on the Arts Literature Program.

NYC Cultural Affairs   NEW YORK STATE OF OPPORTUNITY. | Council on the Arts